Squirrels

Trudi Strain Trueit

Marshall Cavendish
Benchmark
New York

Other Marshall Cavendish Offices:
Marshall Cavendish International (Asia) Private Limited, 1 New Industrial Road, Singapore 536196
Marshall Cavendish International (Thailand) Co Ltd. 253 Asoke, 12th Flr, Sukhumvit 21 Road, Klongtoey Nua, Wattana, Bangkok 10110, Thailand
Marshall Cavendish (Malaysia) Sdn Bhd, Times Subang, Lot 46, Subang Hi-Tech Industrial Park, Batu Tiga, 40000 Shah Alam, Selangor Darul Ehsan, Malaysia

Marshall Cavendish is a trademark of Times Publishing Limited

All websites were available and accurate when this book was sent to press.

Library of Congress Cataloging-in-Publication Data

Trueit, Trudi Strain.
Squirrels / by Trudi Strain Trueit.
p. cm. — (Backyard safari)
Includes bibliographical references and index.
Summary: "Identify specific squirrel species. Explore their behavior, life cycle, mating habits, geographical location, anatomy, enemies, and defenses"—Provided by publisher.
ISBN 978-1-60870-248-0 (print) ISBN 978-1-60870-627-3 (ebook)
1. Squirrels—Juvenile literature. I. Title.
QL737.R68T78 2011
599.36—dc22
2010014800

Expert Reader: Dr. Eric Yensen, Department of Biology, The College of Idaho, Caldwell, ID

Editor: Christine Florie
Publisher: Michelle Bisson
Art Director: Anahid Hamparian
Series Designer: Alicia Mikles

Photo research by Marybeth Kavanagh

Cover photo by Rolf Nussbaumer/NPL/*Minden Pictures*
The photographs in this book are used by permission and through the courtesy of: *Alamy*: PhotoStock-Israel, 4; John Warburton-Lee Photography, 16; Robert Shantz, 23(top L); Rolf Nussbaumer Photography, 23(top R); Rick & Nora Bowers, 23(bottom L); Rhoda Peacher, 23(bottom R); *Photo Researchers, Inc.*: Ed Cesar, 6R; Nick Bergkessel Jr., 19; Millard H. Sharp, 27; *Getty Images*: Philippe Henry/Oxford Scientific, 6L; Jane Burton/Dorling Kindersley, 8; *Minden Pictures*: S&D&K Maslowski/FLPA, 7; *Superstock*: age fotostock, 10, 15, 17; Radius, 11; All Canada Photos, 21, 22(top center); 22 (bottom L); 22 (bottom R); 23(top center); 23 (bottom center); Mark Newman, 22 (top R); Flirt, 26; *Media Bakery*: BigStockPhoto, 13(top R), 13(center R); *Cutcaster*: Nikolaj Kondratenko, 13 (top L); Ivan Montero, 13 (center R); Sergey Skryl, 13 (bottom R); Sergej Razvodovskij, 13 (bottom L); *Animals Animals Enterprises*: Azure Computer & Photo Services, 14; *Dembinsky Photo Associates*: Skip Moody, 22 (top L); *The Image Works*: Hal Beral/V&W, 22 (bottom center); Syracuse Newspapers/M Greenlar, 28; *Ardea.com*: Donald Burgess, 24L; Kenneth W. Fink, 24R

Printed in Malaysia (T)
1 3 5 6 4 2

Contents

Introduction

Have you ever watched baby spiders hatch from a silky egg sac? Or seen a butterfly sip nectar from a flower? If you have, you know how wonderful it is to discover nature for yourself. Each book in the Backyard Safari series takes you step-by-step on an easy outdoor adventure, then helps you identify the animals you've found.

You'll also learn ways to attract, observe, and protect these valuable creatures. As you read, be on the lookout for the Safari Tips and Trek Talk facts sprinkled throughout the book. Ready? The fun starts just steps from your back door!

ONE
Spunky Squirrels

When you see a squirrel bounce past, do you stop to see what this bundle of energy is up to? Squirrels are cute, clever, and curious animals. They are also quite hardy. Squirrels thrive in all kinds of environments, from Alaska's frozen plains to New York's Central Park.

Trek Talk
More than seventy-five different kinds of squirrels live in North America. All of the types live west of the Mississippi River, but only about ten kinds are found east of the Mississippi River.

Life on the Go

Some North American squirrels live in trees, while others make their homes near or under the ground. In warm weather a tree squirrel lives in a **drey** (DRAY), a ball-shaped nest made of leaves, twigs, moss, and other natural materials. It builds its drey in the branches of a tree.

When the weather gets cold, a squirrel may take shelter in a tree hollow, called a den. Ground squirrels, chipmunks, and prairie dogs live in **burrows**. A ground squirrel digs tunnels to create an underground nest with one or more chambers.

A red squirrel attends to her young in a drey she built of leaves, twigs, and other natural materials.

Talented Tails

Squirrel is a Greek word that means "shadow-tailed." It refers to the way a squirrel may use its tail to shade itself from the sun. A squirrel uses its tail for balance as well as a parachute for gliding, a cushion for landing, an umbrella on rainy days, and a blanket on chilly nights. It even uses its tail to communicate. A squirrel flicking its tail is telling other squirrels and animals to stay away from its food or nest.

Ground squirrels tend to live together in groups. Tree squirrels usually live alone (in winter they may snuggle together for warmth until temperatures rise). In late winter a female tree squirrel gives birth to three to five babies. A newborn baby squirrel weighs about as much as a fortune cookie. It is blind and has no fur. Squirrels are **mammals**, like humans, so the mother nurses her young. When the babies are about two months old, their mother begins teaching them how to find food and water, build a nest, and avoid **predators**. In a month or so, the young squirrels are ready to strike out on their own. Squirrels live up to eight years. However, their lives are frequently cut short by predators, starvation, harsh weather, and traffic.

This eastern gray squirrel feeds her young.

Remarkable Rodents

Squirrels are part of a larger group of animals known as **rodents**. This group include mice, rats, hamsters, porcupines, and beavers. The word *rodent* is Latin for "to gnaw," which is what a squirrel spends much of its time doing. All rodents have four **incisors** (two in the upper jaw and two

Squirrels are members of the rodent family. They share similar features with mice and rats.

in the lower). These razor-sharp teeth, along with powerful jaw muscles, make it a snap for a squirrel to crack nutshells. Unlike your teeth, which stop growing when you are a teenager, a squirrel's teeth never stop growing. A squirrel must constantly gnaw to keep its incisors short and sharp.

Safari Tip

Squirrels are big talkers. They **chirr**, or call, to communicate, warn of danger, and scare off predators. Eastern and western gray squirrels often let out a loud *kuk-kuk-kuk* squawk when humans, dogs, or other threats are nearby. Chipmunks make a high-pitched *chip-chip-chip* call, which is how they may have earned their name. Another theory is that the name comes from the Algonquin Indian word *adjidamo*, which means "he who runs with his tail in the air." Go online and listen to audio clips of squirrels to become familiar with their chirring before you go on safari.

The cheek pouches of this eastern chipmunk bulge with seeds.

Squirrels eat nuts, seeds, fruit, pinecone seeds, bark, fungi, birds' eggs, flower bulbs, and plants. Most create a **cache** (KASH), a stockpile of food, for the winter. Some ground squirrels, such as chipmunks, have stretchy cheek pouches that they fill with food to take back to their burrows. Their cheek pouches can hold sixty sunflower seeds at once! If a chipmunk discovers a supply of food, such as a bird feeder, look out. These expert stashers will haul away a gallon of food a day.

As the weather turns cold, some ground squirrels enter a state of light **hibernation**. A squirrel may wake several times during the winter to eat from its cache. Tree squirrels do not hibernate. A tree squirrel prefers to store its cache in various places. It may bury a nut a few inches under the soil, slip one into a tree hollow, and hide another under leaves.

Squirrels have four fingers and a thumb on each paw, making it easy to hold onto objects.

Have you ever noticed that squirrels hold their food the way you do? That's because, like us, squirrels have four fingers and a thumb on each hand. They also have five toes on each foot. However, tree squirrels can do something we can't: swivel their ankle joints so their feet face backward. This is how a squirrel races down a tree face-first without falling.

Squirrels are nimble, speedy creatures. They can leap 15 feet between branches and have been clocked running at 20 miles per hour!

Now that you've had a glimpse into the dizzying world of squirrels, it's time to head out on safari.

TWO

You Are the Explorer

You can safari for squirrels almost any time of the year in North America. In late winter and spring, you are likely to find tree squirrels playfully chasing each other as they choose mates. In spring and summer, squirrels are building dreys and raising their young. In autumn, squirrels will be storing food for the winter. Although ground squirrels hibernate during the winter, tree squirrels remain active (the colder it is, however, the less likely you are to see them out of their dens).

Trek Talk
Your heart beats at around seventy beats per minute, while a squirrel's heart beats up to three hundred times every minute! In hibernation, a ground squirrel's pulse may drop to three beats per minute.

Try to go on safari when the outside temperature is between 50 and 80 degrees Fahrenheit. Choose a day when it isn't raining, snowing, or windy. The best times to go are before 11:00 AM or between 5:00 PM and 7:00 PM (as long as it is still light outside). Please leave your pets at home.

What Do I Wear?

- A hat with a brim
- A long-sleeved shirt
- Jeans or long pants
- Sweater or coat
- Gloves and boots
- Sunglasses
- Sunscreen

What Do I Take?

- Binoculars
- Digital camera
- Notebook
- Colored pens or pencils
- Blanket or towel to sit on
- Handful of unsalted peanuts (optional)
- Water

Safari Tip

It can be fun to feed squirrels corn, sunflower seeds, and unsalted nuts (salted nuts are not healthy for squirrels). Even so, you should never feed them by hand. A squirrel may mistake your finger for a nut, and its teeth are sharp enough to bite to the bone! Try the projects in Chapter 4 to safely feed the squirrels.

Where Do I Go?

Find a spot in your backyard that is attractive to squirrels. They will be looking for:

* Tall trees
* Tree hollows, stumps, and logs
* Vines, spring buds, sunflowers, and flower bulbs
* Water source, such as a birdbath, stream, or creek
* Bird feeders

One of the places squirrels are attracted to are gardens with flowers and flower bulbs.

If your backyard doesn't offer these features, here are some other good safari locations:

- ❋ Woodlands
- ❋ Public parks
- ❋ Zoos
- ❋ Grassy prairies and meadows (ground squirrels)

Always have an adult with you if you are going beyond your backyard.

Crafty Creatures

Squirrels are a daring, determined bunch, especially when the task involves food. They will dangle from the thinnest tree limb or leap several feet to reach bird feeders. One was even caught on video tape slipping inside a vending machine to steal candy. The British documentary *Daylight Robbery* detailed their astounding ability to figure out the most challenging of obstacle courses. The rodents learned to shinny up tubes, spin on a windmill, and ride in a little car down a ramp to reach a bowl of nuts. Want to see it for yourself? Chapter 4 will show you how to make a simple squirrel obstacle course.

What Do I Do?

* If you brought some unsalted peanuts, crack the shells. Place the peanuts beneath a tree or on a stump to attract a hungry squirrel.

* Find a shady spot at least 20 feet from where you put the nuts and sit down. Scan the area with your binoculars. Look for squirrels resting in trees, leaping from limb to limb, or zipping along logs or fences. A squirrel tends to follow the same path as it ventures through its territory, which may be up to 7 acres in size.

* Stay quiet. Tree squirrels are easily spooked, but chipmunks and other ground squirrels are friendlier. If you are quiet and keep still, they may come closer to feed, soak up the sun, or look you over.

When on safari, be sure to sit quietly while watching for squirrels.

Safari Tip

If you see a squirrel with stripes on its face, it's a chipmunk. Chipmunks have two light stripes alternating with three dark stripes across each cheek. They have light and dark stripes on their backs, too. Other types of ground squirrels, such as the golden-mantled ground squirrel and the thirteen-lined ground squirrel, also have stripes on their backs (but not on their faces).

❋ Listen for squirrels chirring. They will trill, chatter, and bark, usually as an alarm. Some squirrels, such as the rock squirrel and the Franklin's ground squirrel, chirp like birds.

❋ When you see a squirrel, snap its photo or do a quick sketch (draw quickly!) in your notebook. Make an entry, too. Describe the color of the squirrel's fur. Look for **field marks**, such as spots and stripes. Note the color, thickness, and where the squirrel is located. What color, size, and shape is the squirrel's tail? If the squirrel is chirring, what does it sound like? Finally, write down a few lines about the squirrel's activities. Did it take the peanuts you left under the tree? Leave a blank line at the bottom of your entry to add its name later.

SQUIRREL

Color (s): mostly gray back, reddish
brown head, white stomach

Field marks: no stripes or spots

Tail: reddish brown and gray,
thick, long

Activity: resting on branch with tail
across back. Squirrel opened and ate an acorn.

Name: _____

Your Drawing or
Photo Goes Here

❋ Spend about a half hour to an hour on safari.
❋ Clean up the area. Take everything but the peanuts with you
when you leave.

Did you have fun on safari? Don't worry if you didn't see any squirrels. Every safari is different. Try again soon. At home, download your photos onto the computer and print them. Move on to the next chapter to discover more about your furry backyard visitors.

Safari Tip

Flying squirrels don't really fly—they glide. These squirrels have special membranes connecting their arms and legs. A flying squirrel launches itself from a tree and spreads its arms and legs, using the membranes like the wings of a hang glider. North America's two types of flying squirrels can soar up to 200 feet! Flying squirrels may take over nest boxes that have been abandoned by birds. These gliding squirrels are night hunters, so look for them close to sunset (hint: they *are* hard to find).

THREE

A Guide to Squirrels

Your outdoor adventure is over, and you're ready to get to work identifying your squirrels. First, select an entry from your notebook. If you took a photo, paste it beside its description. Next, go through the field guide on the following pages. As you compare your squirrel to those in the guide, focus on these areas:

❋ Color: Look at the color of the fur on the squirrel's body, head, and tail.

❋ Field marks: Does your squirrel have spots or stripes? What color are they? Where are they located? Remember, chipmunks are the only squirrels that have striped faces.

❋ Tail: What is its shape and size? Tree squirrels have bushy tails. Chipmunks have thin tails. Prairie dogs and some western ground squirrels have short tails.

When you locate your squirrel, fill in the blank you left in your entry. If you have trouble making a match, don't get discouraged. Identifying squirrels can be difficult. Did you know that some of the same types of squirrels come in different colors? The eastern gray squirrel may be gray, brown, black, or even white! For more help, use the resources listed in the Find Out More section.

SQUIRREL

Color (s): mostly gray back, reddish brown head, white stomach

Field marks: no stripes or spots

Tail: reddish brown and gray, thick, long

Activity: resting on branch with tail across back. Squirrel opened and ate an acorn.

Name: EASTERN GRAY

Squirrel Guide: Ground Squirrels

Eastern Chipmunk

Yellow-pine Chipmunk

Spotted Ground Squirrel

Golden-mantled Ground Squirrel

Black-tailed Prairie Dog

Woodchuck

Squirrel Guide: Tree Squirrels

Abert's Squirrel

Eastern Gray Squirrel

Eastern Fox Squirrel

Western Gray Squirrel

Red Squirrel

Douglas's Squirrel

Squirrel Guide: Flying Squirrels

Southern Flying Squirrel

Northern Flying Squirrel

FOUR

Try This!
Projects You Can Do

It's fun to watch squirrels frolic, but did you know that these friendly, curious animals play an important role on Earth? Squirrels are nature's gardeners. Some of the nuts and seeds they bury grow, becoming new flowers, plants, and trees. Also, as ground squirrels dig their burrows, they bring air, water, and nutrients to the soil. Good soil makes for strong, healthy plants.

Despite their value, many squirrels around the world are losing ground in the fight for survival. Habitat destruction, agricultural pest control programs, hunting, and collection for the pet trade (flying squirrels) are putting them at risk. Our recreational habits are also taking a toll. The U.S. Fish and Wildlife Service says that on some popular mountain peaks, hikers are trampling and destroying the plants squirrels rely on to survive. When in the wilderness, you can help by simply staying on marked trails and leaving the area the way you found it. At home, why not try some of the projects in this chapter? They offer great ways to observe and protect these energetic, furry mammals that share our backyards.

Vanishing Prairie Dogs

Prairie dogs were once a common sight on the western plains of the United States and Canada (pioneers named them for their doglike bark). Yet, in less than 150 years, the population of these ground squirrels, found only in North America, has declined by 95 percent! Some, such as the Utah prairie dog, face **extinction** and are now protected by law. What happened? In the early twentieth century, ranchers began killing prairie dogs, fearing they competed with cattle for food. Studies have disproven this, showing that prairie dogs improve soil quality, provide shelter for other animals, and eat weeds harmful to cattle. Still, many ranchers and governments continue to view these ground squirrels as pests.

Feeding Station

Attract squirrels year-round with this easy-to-make feeder. Find a small clay flowerpot without holes in the bottom. Fill the pot about two-thirds full with cracked corn, shelled unsalted peanuts, and sunflower seeds. Place the pot on an old tree stump or fence post during the day. Bring it in at the end of the day so the food doesn't attract mice and rats over-night. Be patient. It may take a few weeks for the squirrels to discover your feeder, but once they do you'll be kept busy filling it again and again!

Peanut String Obstacle Course

An obstacle course is a great way to feed and observe squirrels. Make a string of peanuts using an old shoelace and five peanuts. Loosely tie each peanut onto the string several inches apart. Hang your peanut string on the end of a tree limb. When squirrels have figured out how to reach the peanuts, add some new twists to your course, such as a ramp or tube (be sure it's wide enough for a squirrel to run through).

Safari Tip

Did you find a baby squirrel on the ground? It probably fell from its drey. Here's what to do: first, put all your pets inside. Then, keep your distance to give the squirrel's mother a chance to come for her offspring. If she doesn't return within three hours, contact your local wildlife rehabilitation center. They will tell you how to safely take the baby squirrel for help.

Nesting Bag

Squirrels are always looking for materials from which to build their wind-proof, waterproof dreys. You can help by creating a nesting bag with some of their favorite items. You'll need a netted produce bag, such as one that holds oranges or onions. Fill it with any combination of the following:

* Twigs or short strips of bark
* Dried leaves
* Moss
* Feathers
* Cotton balls

Tie the bag at the top. Hang it from a sturdy branch. Check the nesting bag every few days. Which items do your squirrels like best? Keep track in your journal.

A gray squirrel collects maple leaves and grass for its nest. You can help out by making a nesting bag for the squirrels in your backyard.

The more you safari for squirrels, the more you'll learn about them, and, amazingly, the more they'll learn about you! After a while some squirrels may even recognize you, especially if you are regularly filling a feeder. Always remember, squirrels are wildlife, not pets. Give them space and respect, and you'll be enjoying these high-energy, high-flying backyard animals for a lifetime.

Glossary

burrows	underground tunnel systems that may or may not contain nests
cache	a hiding place for food
chirr	the vocal calls that some tree squirrels make
drey	a squirrel's ball-shaped tree nest
extinction	the dying out of a particular kind of plant or animal
field marks	spots, stripes, or other distinguishing marks on a squirrel
hibernation	passing the winter in a state of inactivity
incisors	teeth used for cutting or gnawing
mammals	animals that give birth to live babies and nurse their young
predators	animals that hunt other animals for food
rodents	a group of mammals characterized by large incisors, such as squirrels, mice, and beavers

Find Out More

Books

Beer, Amy-Jane. *Chipmunks*. Danbury, CT: Grolier/Scholastic, 2008.

Eder, Tamara. *Squirrels of North America*. Auburn, WA: Lone Pine Publishing, 2009.

Thorington, Richard W., Jr., and Katie E. Ferrell. *Squirrels: The Animal Answer Guide.* Baltimore, MD: The Johns Hopkins University Press, 2006.

DVD and Video

The Life of Mammals Vol. 1–4, BBC Warner, 2008.

BBC: Natural History: Daylight Robbery 2, BBC Home Video, 1995.

Websites

e Nature Field Guide

www.enature.com/fieldguides

Click on "mammals" then "chipmunks," "squirrels," and "prairie dogs" to reach the squirrel field guide, which offers photos and descriptions of the most common North American squirrels.

National Geographic

http://animals.nationalgeographic.com/animals/mammals/squirrel.html

Log on to explore the squirrel photo gallery, print out a fact sheet, and hear the call of the eastern gray squirrel.

The Smithsonian National Museum of Natural History—North American Mammals

www.mnh.si.edu/mna/image_menu.cfm

View images and descriptions of North America's squirrels, chipmunks, prairie dogs, and marmots at this site. Create your own custom squirrel and chipmunk field guide to print out and take with you on your next safari.

Index

Page numbers in **boldface** are illustrations.

Meet the Author

TRUDI STRAIN TRUEIT can't get enough of watching squirrels feed, play, and bury nuts in her backyard. An award-winning journalist, Trudi has written more than sixty fiction and nonfiction books for children on various topics, but writing about nature tops her list. She is the author of four other books in the Backyard Safari series, including *Frogs and Toads*, *Caterpillars and Butterflies*, and *Birds*. Trudi lives in Everett, Washington, with her husband, Bill, a photography teacher (and fellow squirrel lover). Visit her website at www.truditrueit.com.